Exploring Materials

Metal

Abby Colich

Raintree is an imprint of Capstone Global Library Limited, a company incorporated in England and Wales having its registered office at 7 Pilgrim Street, London, EC4V 6LB Registered company number: 6695582

To contact Raintree:
Phone: 0845 6044371
Fax: + 44 (0) 1865 312263
Email: myorders@raintreepublishers.co.uk
Outside the UK please telephone +44 1865 312262

Text © Capstone Global Library Limited 2014
First published in hardback in 2014
The moral rights of the proprietor have been asserted.

Edited by Abby Colich, Daniel Nunn, and Catherine Veitch
Designed by Marcus Bell
Picture research by Tracy Cummins
Production by Victoria Fitzgerald
Originated by Capstone Global Library Ltd
Printed and bound in China by Leo Paper Products Ltd

ISBN 978 1 4062 6332 9
17 16 15 14 13
10 9 8 7 6 5 4 3 2 1

British Library Cataloguing in Publication Data
Colich, Abby.
Metal. – (Exploring materials)
620.1´6-dc23
A full catalogue record for this book is available from the British Library.

Acknowledgements
We would like to thank the following for permission to reproduce photographs: Getty Images pp. 10 (© Robb Kendrick), 14 (© OJO Images); Shutterstock pp. 4 (© Jaimie Duplass), 5 (© danilo ducak), 6 (© Jeanne Hatch), 7a (© Garsya), 7b (© Flashon Studio), 7c (© Shkvarko), 7d (© Kamira), 8 (© Repina Valeriya), 9 (© Jiri Foltyn), 11, 23b (© zmkstudio), 12 (© Luciano Mortula), 13 (© MikeE), 15 (© luiggi), 16 (© portumen), 17 (© oksana.perkins), 18 (© Monkey Business Images), 19, 23a (© MSPhotographic) 20 (© Leah-Anne Thompson), 21 (© Redshinestudio), 22 (© Tom Mc Nemar, © gualtiero boffi, © Volodymyr Krasyuk).

Front cover photograph of a boy playing with magnets reproduced with permission of Getty Images (© Zigy Kaluzny).

Back cover photograph reproduced with permission of Shutterstock (© MSPhotographic).

We would like to thank Valarie Akerson, Nancy Harris, Dee Reid, and Diana Bentley for their assistance in the preparation of this book.

Every effort has been made to contact copyright holders of material reproduced in this book. Any omissions will be rectified in subsequent printings if notice is given to the publisher.

Contents

What is metal?

Metal is a material.

Materials are what things are made from.

There are many different types
of metal.

We use metal for many
different things.

Where does metal come from?

Metal is found in nature.

Metal is found in rock.

People dig for metal in the ground.

Metal can be recycled or used to make new things.

What is metal like?

Some metal is hard and strong.

Some metal can bend and change shape.

Metal can be smooth and shiny.

Metal can be heavy or light.

How do we use metal?

We use metal to build things.

We use metal to make trains, cars,
bicycles, and road signs.

We use metal to make computers.

container

We use metal to make containers.

Some toys are made of metal.

Many things are made from metal.

Quiz

a

b

c

Which of these things are made of metal?

Answer on page 24.

Picture glossary

container something used to store things

recycle make used items into new things

Index

The **watering can (b)** and **fence railings (c)** are made of metal.

Notes for parents and teachers

Before reading

Ask children if they have heard the term "material" and what they think it means. Reinforce the concept of materials. Explain that all objects are made from different materials. A material is something that takes up space and can be used to make other things. Ask children to give examples of different materials. These may include glass, plastic, and metal.

To get children interested in the topic, ask if they know what metal is. Identify any misconceptions they may have. Ask them to think about whether their ideas might change as the book is read.

After reading

- Check to see if any of the identified misconceptions have changed.
- Show the children examples of metal, including toys, cans, and jewellery.
- Pass the metal objects round the children. Ask them to describe the properties of each object. What colour is the metal? Is it heavy or light? Big or small? Ask them to name other items made from metal.